from 308 to F40
Ferrari
V8

Ferrari V8

Beki Adam

Published in 1990 by Osprey Publishing
59 Grosvenor Street
London W1X 9DA

British Library Cataloguing in Publication
Data.
Adam, Beki
   Ferrari V8.
   I. Title   II. Morland, Andrew
   629.2′222

ISBN 0-85045-881-1
Page Design Janette Widdows

Printed in Hong Kong

For a catalogue of all books published by Osprey Automotive
please write to:

**The Marketing Manager, Consumer Catalogue Department
Osprey Publishing Ltd, 59 Grosvenor Street, London, W1X 9DA**

CONTENTS

Above

A symbol of excellence

Page 1

The heart of the matter

Pages 2/3

*Not all Ferraris are red—a 308
quattrovalvole*

As with so many books, many people helped in putting this one together, and the author and publisher would like to extend their sincere thanks to them for that help. Most of the photographs were shot specifically for this book by Andrew Morland; other photographs were supplied by Mirco Decet, *Fast Lane* magazine, Haymarket Publishing, Maranello Concessionaires, Martini Rosso, Quadrant Picture Library and Maurice Rowe. Cars were provided by Greypaul Motors, Ian Harbottle and Martin Hutchings, while locations included Nigel Dawes' Birtsmorton Court and Foster-Yeoman's Torr Works quarry. Finally, we are indebted to the valuable assistance given by Ferrari CEFAC SpA, without which the book would not have been possible.

INTRODUCTION

Italy was alive and buzzing. Every hotel room in the north had been booked—the car world had come to Turin. At the centre of all this attention was Lingotto, the old Fiat factory with its famous roof-top race track. This was to be the venue for Italy's 62nd Motor Show, due to open its doors to the press the following day, Wednesday 20 April 1988. Meanwhile, just a step away from the communal buzz of Turin, I was experiencing a massive buzz all of my own in Maranello, a little town south of Modena.

The announcement and subsequent debut on 27 July 1987 of an extraordinary car, the Ferrari F40, had had the automotive world raising hell for nearly a year. Could this car, created to celebrate the 40th anniversary of Ferrari, the automobile manufacturers, (and co-incidentally the 90th of Ferrari, the man) compete successfully with Porsche's outstanding 959? Could the new Super Ferrari really travel as fast as the factory claimed? And, the most whispered question of them all: was it even in production, and if not, would it ever be?

This was what lensman Andrew Morland and I were trying to find out in Maranello. Porsche had not attained the elusive 200+mph goal, the automotive world was left on tenterhooks, and the stable door wide open. Any horse, prancing or not, could bolt at any second, and this car sounded like it might be the one to do it. The Ferrari F40 was, if nothing else, creating one hell of a stir.

Viewed from outside, the Ferrari factory seems rather plain and ordinary. There are no sprawling lawns with long winding entrance roads to hint of powerful test runs. But there is something in the air. Anticipation.

It would not take long for even the uninitiated to realize they were standing outside the gates of a very important factory, for the premises are not totally incognito. There is a nameboard (and yes, it's yellow), and if you wait long enough, faint rumbles beckon you inside like the Sirens' irresistible call from the rocks. And then, the gates open, and a new 428 or

Any colour you like, so long as . . . .

Only one man builds F40 engines; here he is hard at work

Testarossa appears, pauses for traffic on the busy road, and sneaks off. You're hooked. Before you know it, invitation permitting, you're inside.

You have stepped into a different world. Ferraris are everywhere—this is Utopia. The place is immaculate, and rumours (presumably spread by jealous outsiders) of rusting chassis lined up next to rusting bodyshells of soon-to-be Testarossas, evaporate into thin air.

Through reception, past an early GTO and friends (all red) that sit waiting to greet you; through one of the showroom doors that materialize out of the white walls and then outside again into the heart of it all. Past clutches of bicycles leaning against walls, which provide stark contrast to the ultimate automobiles glinting from every other direction; across sun-bleached concrete—keeping eyes peeled in the painfully

Components for the F40's suspension and braking system

Assembling the cooling system

Above
This equipment supports the rear bodywork while the lights and rear window are installed. The operator can also check that the lights work at the same time

Left
The rear screen doubles as an engine cover and incorporates cooling louvres

11

Rear end of the F40, showing the tubular structure for holding the engine and suspension

reflective brightness for a glimpse of polystyrene and tape-covered creations travelling incognito before production; past yet more Testarossas, Mondials, 308s . . . and into the mainline production complex.

Once inside, there's the recognizable noise of a busy car factory—rattles, hums, bangs, the bursts of riveting—but something's missing. No straining voices fight to be heard above the rattle and hum. There are people, and a lot of them; they just don't need to shout. Everyone knows exactly what they're doing. Everything seems to run to a very refined plan. These quiet, unassuming workers haven't the merest hint of self-importance, yet they work on cars that every materialistic male has dreamt of owning. It's their job that's important, not them. And then there it is. The unmistakable shape, albeit without a front end, of the F40.

An F40 about to undergo final assembly

Pietro De Franchi, Public Relations Manager for Ferrari, says proudly, 'This is the F40, the very best racing sports car'. According to De Franchi, the current production run was set at about 700. Approximately 400 are planned for Europe, with the remainder crossing the Atlantic, where they will somehow pass unnoticed on to America's roads, emission laws or not. The production figure seems to fluctuate dramatically, but if it was to be 700, and, let's face it, the demand's there, then the waiting list will be fairly long, with at most a production rate of two per week. The work sheet for the cars we saw was only up to car number 20.

But there the F40s are, in front of us, and in production. The workers methodically carry out their jobs, starting with basic chassis assembly. The appropriate parts are stored in boxtrays that form a wall down both sides of the actual

production line. Out they come, and on they go. It is a privileged job; F40 workers do not work on any other Ferraris. It really is a very special car. Similarly to Rolls-Royce, each engine is assembled by one man alone. Unlike Rolls Royce, he does not have his name engraved on a brass plaque and stuck on the engine. He has nothing to prove, he does not need this kind of recognition, but above all, he has no

Left
Bodyshell ready for final assembly

Above
The rear end is nearing completion

Below
Coil-overs are used for the rear suspension, and oil coolers are mounted in the wings

The longitudinally-mounted V8 in the F40, showing the air intakes. At this stage, the exhaust has not been fitted

Above
The F40's rear bulkhead, showing the front of the engine and cooling pipes

Left
Gradually a masterpiece takes shape

Front end details show the suspension, braking and steering systems, together with the supporting tubular framework

fellow workers. He is the only man who puts an F40 engine together. Who needs a brass plaque?

Having resisted the temptation to steal the odd nut or bolt, hoping it might bear the hastily designed F40 logo, we move on. De Franchi is with us all the time, answering any questions we may raise, including, 'So how much will it really cost?'

The figure, so large in lire that he hardly knew the English words for it, floated off unheard in the rattle and hum. 'Could you translate that into sterling, please?' I shouted. He tried. As you may have guessed, there was not enough room on his calculator for all the noughts. We did arrive finally at a figure close to £169,000. Ferrari are well aware that there is already a market out there. People lucky enough to be on the original list (drawn up by Ferrari) are selling before they have received. Let's hope they aren't number 699, and let's hope Ferrari don't find out, because they're looking. If they decided to make a car so fast and so powerful that only 'qualified' Ferrari drivers could own one (one has to have owned a **GTO**

*Front-mounted radiator with twin,
thermostatically-controlled cooling fans*

or Testarossa previously), they will not sell cars to people
who will simply pass them on for mega-bucks.

On we moved through various other buildings, the paint
shop, and then the testing area, being passed by an occasional
employee on a bicycle, with its basket full of pistons, plugs
etc. Then, as if someone had turned down a huge volume
control, the rattle and hum seemed to fade away, and a new,
much more beautiful sound, one I'd never heard before,
floated through the air. One of the very first F40s was up and
running. Well, not so much up, just running with two
mechanics literally lying over the back (the engine, please
remember, is large) marking off their test sheets.

Life was suddenly perfect. We were exactly where we
wanted to be; bright sunshine, a running F40, and outside. De
Franchi is a kind man, or just extremely good at his job. He
grabbed one of the first ever F40s, due to be despatched to the
lucky concessionaire, whipped it out from under those
mechanics, and into the open air.

Right
Tuning the F40's engine means lying at almost full stretch

Below right
Here the turbo intercooler is being mounted in the engine compartment

Far right
The F40's turbo intercooler

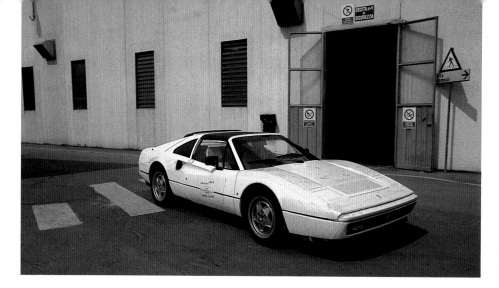

Above
Final tune-up

Top
In the pink. A 308 GTS leaves the production line with its protective plastic coating

His kind thought inconvenienced more than the two disgruntled mechanics. Someone had to be found to drive it, and other cars moved. It may be that De Franchi knew he wouldn't be put under this kind of pressure again, for Ferrari plan to stop all factory visits, especially those of a photographic nature. They get over 1000 requests a day! From lowly British journos, to American schoolkids and proud new owners, everybody wants to have a look around, and Ferrari feel that if you can't keep everybody happy, it's difficult to justify making the effort for some. They employ staff on Saturdays just to show guests around—and they really do lose

The ultimate in the Ferrari V8's evolutionary process—the F40

In fact, I believe the prancing horse has already bolted. Porsche have proved with the 959 that they can create the ultimate in engineering excellence, but without being able to say exactly why, Ferrari's F40 seems to have left Porsche the depressing job of shutting the stable door.

SEPTEMBER 1989

How could I have felt so strongly about a mere piece of machinery? How can a car create such passionate feeling? I've often tried with many of my contemporaries to pinpoint what it is that Ferrari cars do to even the most level-headed of us. *Road Test* once commented, 'Ferrari is as much a legend as it is a company, there is substance and there is myth and it is difficult to discover where one ends and the other begins.' I agree. A red Ferrari waved in front of man has the same effect as a red flag to a bull. That's the real power behind Ferraris.

As such emotive power is impossible to explain, I've

*No matter which way you look at it, the
F40 has winning, race-bred styling*

realized that whatever I write is of secondary importance.
Let's face it, would you rather look at a page full of copy, or a
Ferrari? I hope that you agree with the proportions of the
copy/camera mix, and that rather than thirst for more details
of rubber compounds, you can be refreshed every time you
turn the page—for there will lie another beautiful glossy
photo of a Ferrari.

So that I'm not totally obsolete. I will try to tell the story of
Ferrari's secondary power—their engines, and in particular,
the evolution of the Ferrari V8. For many years, the Ferrari
name has been synonymous with huge V12s. That has now
changed. Since the Dino 308 GT4 of the 1960s, their first V8-
engined production car, the neat little V8 powerplant has
been used in an increasing number of production models.
Now it rumbles beneath the perspex hood of the ultimate
road car. What better reason to write a book on Ferrari V8
engines and their evolution?

A LANCIA-POWERED FERRARI

Tracing the origins of Ferrari's first V8-engined car is fairly complicated. It involves as much to-ing and fro-ing as the pistons in a Boxer. For a start, the car wasn't really a Ferrari at all, it was a Lancia!

Alberto Ascari had previously driven for Ferrari, but in February 1954 he and his team-mate Villoresi had joined Gianni Lancia in the first of many defections from Ferrari. In 1948 Gianni had taken control of Lancia from its founder, his father, Vincenzo. Gianni loved motor racing, and under his command, Lancia would concentrate on Grand Prixs, and thus build a Formula I car for the first time.

This may seem a daunting prospect, but building an FI car for the first time has its advantages—especially if other companies have done the groundwork for you which, of course, they had. In 1954 there was another advantage; the rules for FI cars had just been altered dramatically. To build a car to meet them would be a lot more successful than simply reworking an old idea to fit the bill. Early 1954 had seen Lancia fire up their new V8, the work of their gifted chief designer, Vittorio Jano. Fortunately, it fitted the new rules perfectly. Basically they looked around at other FI cars in action at the time, filched the best ideas, and added their own touch of magic, with the new rules in mind. Lancia were also alone in their choice of engine; they were planning to run a V8, and although Mercedes were to run a straight-8, Ferrari meanwhile were still relying on half that amount of cylinders.

Jano wanted his car to be powerful, nimble, and light. The result, the D50, was a relatively small FI car: 'In essence, the D50 was a means of carrying an engine, gearbox, and a driver as fast as possible through a complex set of manoeuvres in the horizontal plane.'

An intricate, short-wheelbase, space-frame chassis was designed, with the inspired idea of fuel tanks being mounted between the front and rear wheels. Thus, as the race continued and fuel was used, the handling capabilities of the

Fangio at the Belgian Grand Prix in 1956 driving a gift horse—the V8-engined D50, originally developed by Lancia and subsequently handed to Ferrari. The Lancias were superior to Ferrari's own efforts

car did not alter, as with rear-mounted tanks. The pannier-style twin tanks, mounted either side of the car, made the D50 instantly recognizable. Another radical alteration to the basic F1 theme included a diagonally-mounted engine, set at an angle to the mid-line, which dictated that the propellor shaft would run diagonally and, therefore, the driver would sit beside, and not above the propshaft—an aerodynamically advantageous position.

Almost a year of experiment preceded the D50's racing debut, as the advanced design of the car showed its drawbacks in unforeseen development problems. Finally, on 19 October 1954, Gianni gave the green light, and the D50, Ascari and Villoresi (both recently arrived from Ferrari), and the rest of the team set off for Barcelona, and its first race. The problems, including the D50's quirky handling characteristics (it would lose track adhesion at the most peculiar points) had, they hoped, finally been solved.

With all eyes on the D50 during the Barcelona warm-ups, Ascari and Villoresi easily set the best times. Unfortunately, only two laps into the race, Villoresi retired with brake problems. Ascari was ahead by an amazing 20 seconds by lap 9, but eventually retired with a badly slipping clutch. Those ugly

29

development problems had not gone away. Hawthorn took the triumph of winning the last race of the year in his Ferrari. The D50 had arrived and proved it was going to be trouble, but it was already time to prepare for 1955.

No one could have foretold what an incredibly tragic year 1955 would be. It began with the Buenos Aires GP in January. With the temperature over 44°C, the race commenced, but the excessive heat did not suit the Lancias. Neither of them finished, and the honours went to the cooler Fangio, his Mercedes coping better with the scorching track.

The D50's first victory came in the next race, held in Turin. Ascari was first, Villoresi third, and their team-mate Castellotti was fourth. The eighth of May arrived, along with the Naples Grand Prix, the D50s won again, taking first and third. Time, although no one realized, was running out. Monaco was next, with four D50s qualified. Stirling Moss, who had been in the lead, blew up his engine, but was unhurt. This news had not reached Ascari, who was hurtling round a corner, Moss in mind. He roared out of the tunnel, into a chicane (much too fast), and out through a nearby pile of straw bales, over the edge, and into the blue Mediterranean. Ascari and his D50 disappeared in 15 ft of water. A few seconds of silence followed, and then he, and his lucky blue helmet, bobbed back up again.

Ascari was a superstitious man. He always wore that same crash helmet. He also never raced on the 26th of any month— the date on which his father had died behind the wheel. The salt-encrusted D50 was drained off, overhauled, and prepared for the Belgian GP in June, while Ascari was at home, convalescing from his impromptu dip. It was Thursday 26 May, when he suddenly decided to visit Monza, where his team-mates were out practising. Castellotti was there in a 750S Ferrari, and when he pulled in, Ascari asked to borrow his helmet. It appears he had decided, on the spur of the moment, to test the Ferrari himself. The comment was later made that he had not been himself that day, the 26th. In borrowed helmet, Ascari set off round the track at moderate speed. No one is quite sure exactly what happened, but Ascari died as a result of the injuries he sustained in an inexplicable accident. There was nothing wrong with the car, and his ability behind the wheel was unquestioned. The cause was not important. Alberto Ascari was dead; Italy had lost a hero, and motor racing its world champion.

Within days, Lancia had announced their intention to retire

Another D50 at the 1956 Belgian GP, this time driven by Frene. That year the Ferrari drivers went on to win the World Championship with the Ferrari/Lancias

from motor racing. Sadly, it was not just grief that stopped them, although they were, like the rest of the world, shattered by the death of one of motor racing's greatest drivers. Castellotti did actually race in Belgium, in the Mediterranean D50 in honour of Ascari, but on the 17th lap it all ended—the gearbox on the D50 disintegrated—as did Lancia's racing career.

On 7 July 1955, Lancia, influenced by the Italian Automobile Club, announced that, in the interests of Italian motor racing, their F1 cars would be handed over to Automobili Ferrari. Less than three weeks later, six D50s, plus spares, tools, equipment, and even the people, Castellotti and Jano included, were literally handed over. Jano, as a Lancia expert, found himself in an almost foreign camp. Lancia's gift was not greeted with much enthusiasm by Enzo and his staff. After all, by their acceptance, they were acknowledging that in all their time competing in Formula 1, they had not been as successful in creating a winning car as Lancia had done first time around. Lampredi, Ferrari's chief designer took Jano's arrival as a personal insult, which it was—his Squalos simply weren't as good as Jano's D50. Within a very short time Lampredi had bolted the stables, and resurfaced at Fiat.

So, through a series of strange events, Ferrari had their first V8-engined car. The D50s, however, were not to prove such a great success in Ferrari's hands. They had been designed to run on Pirelli tyres, and the Englebert tyres they were now obliged to use shed their tread all over the track. The Belgian tyre reps had no intention of waiving their exclusive Ferrari contract, so the D50s were slowly replaced by Ferrari's original F1 cars, the Super (but probably inferior) Squalos.

Most would agree, with hindsight, that the Lancia D50 showed more promise than the Ferrari D50 with all its minor alterations (including the fairing-in of the pannier fuel tanks). Had Jano been allowed to continue his project, it is generally considered that the car would have stood the test of time. Having said that, however, I must point out that in 1956 the Ferrari drivers, headed by Fangio, won the World Championship in the D50s. Fangio himself won the driving honours, but to be truthful, the competition wasn't exactly stiff.

Development of the four-year-old engine was still proceeding, but it was becoming obvious that 275 bhp was about the most this particular V8 could handle. 7 April 1957 saw the emergence of a revamped D50, along with a name change to the Ferrari 801. Although they continued to race the new-name, old-design 801 during 1957, it did not win a single GP.

The rumble of a V8 clothed in Ferrari racing colours was not heard again until five years later in 1962. This year also saw both BRM and Cooper-Climax running V8s. Sebring saw the debut of Ferrari's brand-new V8, a short-lived, almost experimental car, named the 248 SP. It was an sohc design of 2458 cc giving 250 bhp. They went for a multi-bar chassis, with independent suspension on all four, and an identical body to the earlier model, the 246 SP (a V6).

Their new V8 lasted only one hour at Sebring. By the following race, the Targa Florio, Ferrari had stroked it to 71 mm for 2644 cc, and it was now the 268 SP. Although it was prepared for Phil Hill, he didn't drive it in the Targa. While driving it during testing, the throttle jammed open, and Hill was designated a non-starter—as was the 268. The rapid appearance and disappearance of these two cars suggests that at that time Ferrari were only toying with the V8 idea.

The next V8-engined Ferrari to appear was again a GP car. No 'eight' configuration had impressed anyone enough to qualify for production-car status—this was still dominated by the huge V12s. The 158 SP was a Bellei-developed four-cam giving 1487.5 cc. The chassis, semi-monocoque, was tailor-made for the new engine, which was sufficiently rigid to be used as a fully stressed member—an idea taken from the semi-stressed **D50**. As a derivative of the **156**, the new **V8** was known as the **158**. It was driven almost exclusively through the year by Ferrari's British driver John Surtees and the Italian driver Bandini. It made its debut at the Syracuse **GP**, the first race of the 1964 World Championship season, with Surtees behind the wheel.

It won, with Bandini in the **V6** coming in second. In the next race at Monaco, Surtees only was in a **V8**. Bandini was driving the **156**, its six-cylinder elder brother, and when he failed to finish, both drivers turned up in **158**s at the Dutch **GP**, where results were better.

Results for the rest of the year saw a Ferrari hat-trick, starting with the German **GP** held at the Nürburgring. Surtees, familiar with the track due to his motorbike experience, lapped up the curvaceous course, and took the **158** to another victory. Bandini, driving the **V6**, took the honours at the next race in Austria, and Surtees, back in the **V8**, made it three wins on Ferrari's turf at the Italian **GP**. But already the little **V8**'s days were numbered—Bandini was driving Ferrari's new flat-**12**

The US **GP** saw two **V8**s for Surtees, a flat-**12** for Bandini, and the old **V6** for Rodriguez. All these cars were raced in blue and white instead of Ferrari red, as they were entered by the **North American Racing Team**. Enzo's Italian temperament had again clashed with the regulating bodies in racing. Surtees' car spun, and he came in second, with one race left to regain points for the World Championship honours. In Mexico, he and the **158** came second, and he won the coveted Championship by one point! The same event, only one year later, was the first with no **V8**-powered Ferraris on the grid. The **V8**s had been phased out and replaced by the flat-**12**s.

This time, the **V8**'s absence from the track was to be for good. It has been replaced almost exclusively by 12 cylinders, first in flat form, and then vee; the only exception to this rule are the turboed **V6**s. For the story to continue, the **V8**s would have to rear their rumbling heads on the production line. When the transfer from track to road happened, it was a point of no return. So far, there has never been, nor is there likely to be, a year of Ferrari production without a **V8**. The car that started this irreversible trend was the **308 GT4**.

THE DINO/BERTONE 308 GT4

The development of the 308 GT4, Ferrari's first V8-engined production car, can be traced back a few years before its launch, to a car called the Dino. Named in honour of Enzo's son, who died tragically at the age of 24, the Dino was a fitting start to a story that led on from the 308 GT4, to the 308 GTB, via the 288 GTO, on to the GTO Evoluzione and finally culminated in the F40.

By 1973, Ferrari's road-car production had split into two main categories. These were the front-engined V12 2+2s (so named because you couldn't really call them four-seaters) and the two-seater coupés and Berlinettas that were often used in GT racing—most were dual-purpose (road and track), such as the Dinos. When GT rules changed in 1964, it became almost impossible for the two categories to be combined in any successful formula, so Ferrari coupés and Berlinettas became exclusively road cars, a decision unchanged to this day.

The first Dino, a 2 litre V6 Grand Tourer, was produced in 1967, and known as the 206 GT. In 1969, it was superseded by the 246 GT, a 2.6 litre V6, which was joined in 1972 by a convertible version, the 246 GTS. The V6 Dinos were almost identical. In power, the 206s gave 180 bhp at 8000 rpm, and the 246s gave 195 bhp at 7600 rpm. Both the chassis were made of tubular steel, while the body of the 206 was light alloy, and the 246 steel. Both had unequal wishbones and Weber carbs. But more important than all these facts and figures is the way the Dino looked. Stunning.

Designed by Pininfarina, possibly the greatest Italian design house, the Dino's shape was based heavily on the swooping lines of its racing predecessors. The design was very different to the trends at the time.

The supercar market of the early 1970s was fierce. Lamborghini were producing the Urraco, a 2.5 litre V8; Maserati the Merak, a 3 litre V6; and Porsche with their 2.4

Sharp-edged styling is the work of Bertone

The 2+2 design initially met with resistance from enthusiasts, but the press gave good reviews

litre 911 were already streets ahead. All the cars were 2+2s, and none of them looked anything like the Dino. Automotive design was, and still is, being straightened out—wedge being the operative word. Gone are those beautiful curves.

Even by the end of the 1960s, the scene had been set. The Dino, a car being launched for the 1970s, had the look of the swinging sixties. Ferrari had produced a car that looked dated compared with its contemporaries. A dangerous risk, but it worked.

As the years passed though, it became obvious that a replacement was needed. Porsche's 911 had often been compared with, and beaten, the 246. Ferrari needed a new car, and its successor also had to run on a different engine; they wanted a 3 litre car and they also wanted a 2+2. With emission regulations to consider, Ferrari knew it would be

impossible to beef up the **V6** to carry a heavier and larger **2+2** body without breaking the new laws, so the scene really was set for the production debut of a **V8**. Interestingly (and some say sadly), when Ferrari came to add a **V8** to the **Dino** series, they did not choose their tried and trusted friends at Pininfarina to carry out the design work, but Bertone, another Italian design house, who were Pininfarina's main competition at the time.

Ferrari have never explained that decision, but many have guessed. One of the simplest explanations offered was Pininfarina's busy schedule at the time, others say that Fiat, having just taken over Ferrari, used their influence and old association with Bertone. Whatever the reason, it was obvious that the design house had changed when the Dino 308 GT4 made its lukewarm debut at the Paris Salon in 1973.

Hidden in the GT4's engine compartment is a 3 litre twin-cam. This was the first road-going Ferrari to have a V8 engine

Above
Ian Harbottle's GT4 was one of the last built, and when he found it in Northern Ireland it had covered very few miles indeed

Right
The GT4 displays very angular lines, unlike the later V8 Ferraris

If the debut was lukewarm, the reception was decidedly cool. The new body, built by Scaglietti, was angular and wedge-shaped, and in stark contrast indeed to the swooping curves of the 246s. Immediately the 'little' Ferrari had gone from looking distinctly different to looking almost the same (to the inexperienced eye) as its close rivals. The 'big' Dino had arrived, and it wasn't very popular. It should be understood, for Bertone's sake, that they had been given an unenviable task—to make a 2+2 out of a two-seater, with only an extra 8 in. to play with in the wheelbase. The 2+2 car

always poses a problem. How seriously do you take those two rear seats, and how much styling and art do you sacrifice to ensure practicability and rear passenger comfort? Ferrari sacrificed very little. In fact, if it wasn't for Fiat's blatant intervention and insistence that Ferrari make a car capable of challenging the sophisticated Porsche, then those two rear seats would have been given, if possible, even less attention.

The 308 GT4 was instantly dismissed by many as 'not a real Ferrari'. But, if it's built in Maranello and has a prancing horse on its nose with Enzo's approval, then of course it's a real Ferrari. Nevertheless, the public reaction had its impact. After all, Ferrari had increased production levels dramatically, and they needed to sell all these extra cars. Over the next couple of years they altered many small details on the GT4, most aimed at increasing sales in the US market. Most noticeably, the lower bodywork was painted matt black, a spoiler was added at the front, and both sets of bumpers, which in US spec had protruded considerably, were tamed and tidied. Most importantly, the Dino script was removed from the nose and subtly replaced by a prancing horse, an indication that changes on a bigger scale were underway. Ferrari GT4s with these alterations are sometimes known as 'Series 2'.

The general layout of the 308 was exactly the same as the original Dino. Starting at the front came the spare wheel and radiator, then the passenger compartment, closely followed by the engine, transmission, and rear axle.

The GT4's engine, the new 3 litre 90-degree V8 twin-cam, called the Type F106, had a bore and stroke of 81 × 71 mm, giving a capacity of 2926.9 cc. The engine had a power output of 255 bhp at 7700 rpm. Cylinder block and crankcase were combined using a light alloy casting. Removable cast-iron wet cylinder heads were used, as were cast-iron valve seats. The valves, operating in hemispherical combustion chambers, sat at 46 degrees to each other—just one for inlet, and one for exhaust. They were opened by bucket-type tappets, and were closed by double helical springs. The toothed belt (one per bank) used to drive the cams on each head came straight from the 4.4 litre 365 Boxer.

Underneath the engine, the crankcase was boxed off in a

Posed in an idyllic setting at Nigel Dawes' Birtsmorton Court, a 308 GT4 belonging to a member of the Ferrari Owners' Club

unit in which the front half acted as the oil sump, while the rear half housed the gearbox and limited-slip differential. Cooled water, which had been driven forward by a single-belt pump to the radiator was returned to the rear of the car to begin its job via piping ducted into the centre of the chassis. The chassis itself was typically Ferrari and remarkably strong. In front and behind the rectangular central section, which was made up of oval tubes, there were cross-braced frameworks of angled tubes which held the engine and all-round independent suspension in place.

Ferrari have never needed to advertise, but they did offer

Above
This full red leather interior was an optional extra

Left
Ian Harbottle gets the pleasure of sitting in this seat

the GT4 to the press for road tests. This had never been done before—all previous tests were carried out on privately-owned cars. Ferrari had realized that if the public were, in their ignorance, shaking heads just because the GT4 looked wrong, then at least they could rely on the press to drive the thing—and they knew what an initiated reaction would be.

Motor reported the V8 as 'amazingly flexible and docile ... in fact the engine will pick up cleanly in fifth down from 1000 rpm (25 mph) and soar right up to the maximum speed of 152 mph without any flat spots or cam effects being felt.' *Motor Sport* felt the same way; 'the torque and flexibility of the V8 is quite wonderful'. *Car* added '... and what power there is in the engine. You expect performance from a Ferrari, but this V8 comes as a surprise because not only is it mail-fisted, but its power is spread over an enormous rev range.'

With respect to handling, however, the press weren't so impressed. However, they couldn't really find fault with this as both they and Ferrari knew that the 308 would end up in the hands of many novice Ferrari drivers due to increased production. *Motor* said, 'When cornering, the typical Ferrari understeer is evident, but the faster you go, the less it becomes, and there is a reassuring feeling of stability and safety in fast corners taken near the limit ... but some of the inherent agility of this by no means light car (2930 lb with a full 17.5 litre tank) is lost by the low-geared steering; the expert deplores it, but it may just be as well for the normal consumer'. It is worth mentioning that a spirited use of the gear lever would quickly bring back the pleasures of any unleashed Ferrari. The reported performance figures were impressive—60 mph from standstill in 6.9 seconds, 0–100 in 18.1, and a quarter mile in 14.9.

The decision to make the GT4 available for test had paid off; the write-ups confirmed that the car would stay. So, after semi-successfully overcoming predictable enthusiast resistance to the new engine configuration and radical exterior design, the GT4 was seen as the perfect base for a 308 series. A year after its launch, production of the 246s ceased and the way was paved for the emergence of a new model range (and hopefully a new shape), the 308s.

A GT4 being put through its paces at Castle Coombe

THE PININFARINA 308 GTB

The first official announcement that the **GT4** was to be replaced came in September 1975. For once, Ferrari seemed willing to take a public step-down and call in their old friends, Pininfarina. The 308 **GT4** was to undergo a major design overhaul, and the job was theirs. Enthusiasts and casual observers alike waited with bated breath; one thing for sure, this new **308** was going to look decidedly prettier than its predecessor.

The launch was held in October of the same year at the Paris Salon. No one argued with the fact that it did look prettier, but again to be fair to Bertone, Pininfarina had gone back to a two-seater, not the nightmarish 2+2 arrangement that Bertone had had to cope with. The **GTB** wheelbase had thus reverted to the 246 length, 8 in. shorter than the **GT4**. But, from the swooping plunging nose, past those distinctive conical side-scoops (one for the oil cooler, one for the air filter) to the neatly leveled-off rear end, the line was back in place.

Pininfarina had relished the job, and excelled themselves; the look remains timeless, even today. The mix between the original Dino styling (those side-scoops and the recessed rear concave window), and the 365 **GT4** Berlinetta Boxer (that spliced from bumper-to-tail bodywork, that wonderful nose and equally delightful rear-end with its sail panels extending from the roofline down to the whisper of a spoiler) was styling perfection. The lines are faultless.

Probably the best reflection of the differing styles of the **GT4** and the **GTB** (or Bertone and Pininfarina) are best highlighted in the rear lights of both cars. On the **GT4** they're angular, almost rectangular in fact, and on the **GTB** there are four perfect circles. Pininfarina's lines curve!

A development of the 308, the 328 is similar in appearance to the earlier model, but it has a larger-capacity engine

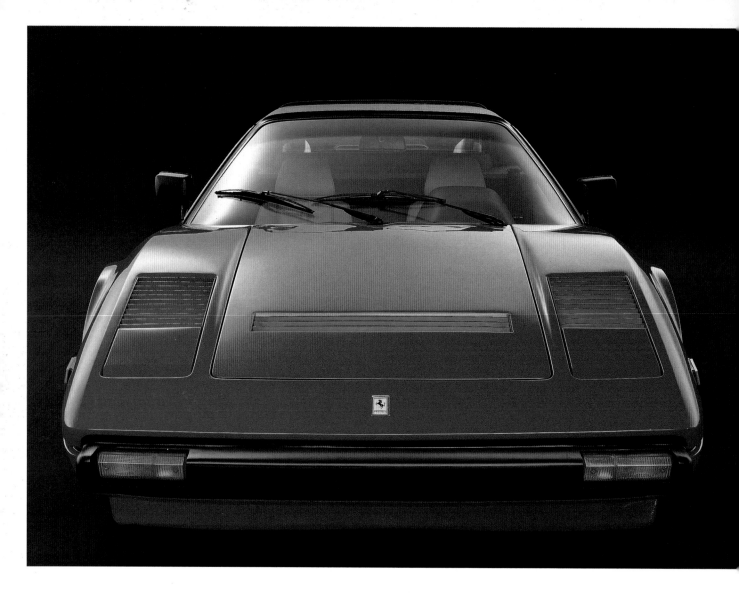

After the disappointment of the GT4, many enthusiasts welcomed the arrival of the 308 GTB. The shapely body was the work of Pininfarina

Probably the next biggest difference was Pininfarina's choice of material for the body—fibreglass. The GTB was the first Ferrari to utilize such a modern material for a complete body. Some say Ferrari wanted a replacement for the GT4 so quickly that 'glass was chosen; production methods were faster—one needs dies for steel, but only nice 'n' easy moulds for 'glass. I'm not so sure that's the reason myself. I think Ferrari knew the GT4 hadn't been such a mistake, despite the public's slow uptake (again) of new ideas. The reason, I believe, was simple; to overcome the rust that plagued the 246s, and to gain advantageous weight reduction.

The engine and transmission were the same as the GT4, a 90-degree V8 with four double-choke Weber carbs mounted between the heads. An electric fuel pump, which drew from the left of twin-tanks, fed fuel to the carbs. A connecting pipe runs between the tanks, and a filter sits between both tank and pump, and pump and carbs, just like the GT4. This engine, the Type F106, which had been introduced on the GT4, was later superseded by the F105, a four-valve unit used on the 328s. All-round independent suspension on both 308s consisted of upper and lower fabricated steel wishbones, coil springs and double-acting hydraulic shock absorbers, with

The 1983 models of the 308 appeared with the quattrovalvole engine with four valves per cylinder

Overleaf
Posed outside Birtsmortan Court is an early 308 belonging to a Ferrari Owners' Club member

49

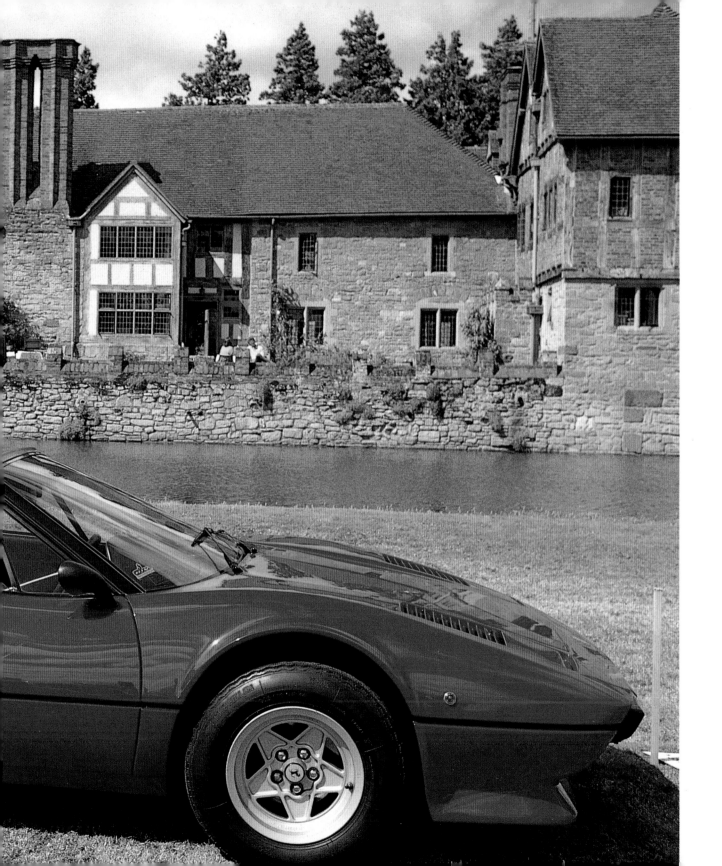

Above
Stylish from any angle

Right
*Rear end treatment of the 328 GTS shows
the brilliant work of Pininfarina*

Above
The classic lines of the 328 set into sharp relief by the rugged terrain of Foster-Yeoman's Torr Works quarry

Left
The GTS provides the best of both worlds—hard top or topless style

Above
Pop-up lights are functional

Right
Also at the Ferrari Owners' Club meeting at Castle Coombe was this modified 308

anti-roll bars fitted at each end. Also, the **US GTBs** retained the four exhaust outlets of the **GT4**, whereas the European models made do with a single outlet on the left of the car. However, they did have the benefits of dry-sump lubrication, while the **US** was left with the less satisfactory wet sump of the **GT4** .... All fair in love and Ferraris.

The standard interior was leather, but the fascia reflected light badly. It's interesting that this long-running Ferrari problem has only just been resolved with the **F40**'s grey-felt interior.

Since the car was so similar to the **GT4**, the press reaction was predictably favourable, especially with the additional benefits of the lighter body and better styling.

Car '.... the feeling of sheer security imparted by the car when it is flat-out through a bend or being thundered through a dip .... It has more of a softness about it than the **308 GT4**, a gentleness; even more poise .... you can really push open the long-travel throttle and let the **V8** propel you forward at a most pleasing rate .... This one is a jewel, an absolute honey; a fun car par excellence.'

Autocar, however, warned any would-be novice owners. 'While the natural tendency is to understeer, if the accelerator is released in the mid-corner the resultant weight transfer does lead to an immediate tightening of the line. This is, of course, no penalty under most conditions (and can be

Below
An early 308 GTB being let off the leash at Castle Coombe circuit

Overleaf
Originally the beautifully styled body of the 308 GTB was manufactured in fibreglass, but within two years the company had reverted to steel for most of the shell

To overcome tax laws in Italy, where the
sales tax on new cars with engines over
2 litres is double that on those with engines
below that capacity, Ferrari introduced
2 litre versions of the GTB, known as the
208. Unfortunately, performance dropped
as a result and sales suffered. The solution
was turbocharging, using a single KKK
unit together with Bosch K-Jetronic fuel
injection. This arrangement gave 220 bhp
at 7000 rpm—approximately the same as
the fuel-injected 308s

used to advantage), but some caution is needed on wet or
slippery roads.'

As with the **GT4**, it would be better to drive the **GTB**
knowing a little of Ferrari characteristics, but the general
reaction to the GTB was better from the outside, and better
from behind the wheel. The weight reduction gained with the
loss of the +2 'rear seats' and, for a time, the fibreglass body
helped the little V8 tremendously.

Both models continued to enjoy good public and press
reactions. The 308 GTB was everything the 308 GT4 had been
(except for a 2+2), plus a lot more. In 1977 the **GTB** was
joined, in true Ferrari tradition, by the **GTS**, the Spyder that
seems to join all successful production models— and from
that year on, both were made with predominantly steel

Comfortable interior of the 328 GTS

bodies, although the floorpan and lower body panels were left in 'glass (see what I mean about the rust). The probable reason for this semi-reversion to steel was the actual production problems experienced with fibreglass manufacture. Ultimately, fibreglass production isn't much quicker—production levels had fallen behind schedule—or cheaper, with repairs especially problematic.

The next step in the car's evolution was to add fuel-injected versions, the 308 GTBi and GTSi, in 1981. Bosch K-Jetronic fuel injection was fitted to combat ever stiffening emission laws, specifically in the US. Ferrari also decided to upgrade the ignition system to an electronic Marelli Digiplex, improve the clutch operation, modify the gearbox and pump-drive its lubrication. They also changed the European models back to

wet-sump main lubrication, in line with the US models, installed a better exhaust system, redecorated the interior in Connolly, and fitted Michelin TRX tyres.

The advantages of fuel injection, other than cleaner fumes, are more uniform combustion, no fuel starvation on the tilt, a better chance of starting on those cold winter mornings, and less chance of waking the neighbours when you do. Little else on the car changed, except of course for an 'i' appearing at the end of the rear script.

Car commented, 'What the Michelins seem to do is to dramatically cut the old car's low-speed tyre noise and to further "tune" the chassis breakaway characteristics so that they are utterly predictable and quite graceful .... The throttle pedal controls it all. It is a little lighter than the one which in previous models controlled a bank of Webers, but just as sensitive.' *Road and Track* added, 'This is not a car for the novice to drive on a winding, slippery road because it does not reward indecision.'

At this point, if we were to continue following the direction of this chapter, it would take us into the world of taxation, the 208, the Turbo, and the Mondial. Do not fret, all will receive fair mention, but their relevance to our ultimate destination is limited. We must, therefore, jump sideways, while production runs of the 308 series continue unabated, and take a look at the GTOs.

The 328 GTS features a refined front end treatment when compared to the earlier 308

A styling exercise by Pininfarina on their own handiwork, an early 308

Side view of the restyled 308, showing new side panels

Overleaf
'Qv' versions of the 308 are distinguished by the 'quattrovalvole' script on the rear panel

THE GTO EVOLUTION

The names Ferrari and GTO are synonymous, like the prancing horse and its yellow background. The two great automotive names first came together in 1962 when Ferrari launched the stunning 250 Gran Tourismo Omologato. As its title might suggest, this car was a racer, designed to compete (and win) in the Manufacturers International Championship, now known as the World Sports Car Championship. It would, therefore, have to be homologated—a process that normally required a production run of 100, although Enzo in his inimitable style got away with only 40. Apart from the GTO suffix, the 250 is really quite unconnected with its successor, the 288, but together they demonstrate a transition that has taken place under the hood of many a Ferrari. In 1962 the 250 GTO was powered by a 3 litre V12, whereas the 288 ran, as you might expect, on a neat little V8.

Both cars were designed with the primary objective—speed. Although the later 288 was not built for competition, the 250 was, and it underlined the point in the 1960s by winning almost every race it finished. It was first in class and second overall at Le Mans in 1962 and 1963, and similarly at the Nürburgring in 1963 and 1964, to name but a few. The 250 is only briefly mentioned as its relevance to our story is limited—and, just to annoy the enthusiasts, it was a bit of a flash in the pan anyway! Enzo's opinion was that few drivers would be capable of controlling such a powerful machine, so the fact that only 40 were built was of little worry to him. Much to the impatience of sportscar lovers worldwide, he was happy to leave it at that for over 20 years.

The GTO's flowing lines owe much to the style of the 308 GTB

Overleaf
Pininfarina were responsible for styling the GTO and produced a swoopy, aerodynamic shape, making considerable use of modern composite materials

Designed with speed as its primary objective, the 288 GTO is, nevertheless, a beautiful car

Then, at last on 1 March 1984 at Geneva, the new 288 GTO arrived. One on the Ferrari stand, and one on Pininfarina's.

The 288 was beautiful. Pininfarina obviously relished the idea of reflecting and complementing the almost faultless lines of their 308 GTB, the car on which this new GTO was obviously based, as much as they had enjoyed creating the GTB after the angular GT4.

The new body was the work of Dr Leonardo Fioravanti, Director-General of Pininfarina Studi e Recherche SpA. He and his team actually cut up a GTB, and kept adding bits—the new GTO had a wheelbase 11 cm longer than the GTB. The rear door jambs and wheelarches are recalled as being most problematic. But, as usual, Pininfarina did a beautiful job, and also found plenty of scope for improved aerodynamics. Extensive use of weight-saving Kevlar and other carbon-fibre

The limited-production GTO is always an attention getter

composite materials made sure that the car weighed in at only 1220 kg, and continued Ferrari's use of modern technology to keep their cars at the front of the field.

Giovanni Squazzini, Ferrari's managing director at the time, explained, 'the concept throughout was to increase power and reduce weight'. The wheelbase extension was done to accommodate the V8 and its transmission in-line, replacing the previous transverse GTB mounting. This directional change allowed the engine to be dropped 7 cm lower than previously, giving a much better centre of gravity. The twin-

71

Far left
The 288 GTO appeared in 1984, over 20 years after the original competition 250 Gran Turismo Omologato had coined the GTO title

Above
Lengthening the wheelbase in comparison with the GTB not only allowed the engine to be mounted longitudinally, but also lower in the car to keep the centre of gravity low

Left
A purposeful road car, the GTO is capable of reaching 60 mph from a standing start in five seconds and can turn 180 mph

turbo engine was not the Type 105/6 from the 308 series, but a direct descendant of the 268 C V8 turbo produced by Ferrari in 1983 for Lancia's LC$\frac{1}{2}$ endurance racing coupés.

The 90-degree V8 produced 400 bhp and was mounted so far forward that its front four cylinders actually lay ahead of the rear screen line. It's interesting to note that the twin-turbos came from Japan. The 288 was fitted with a new Weber-Marelli electronic engine management system. This digitally controlled fuel mixture, etc, with overall control being divided into two, one per bank. The steel-tube chassis was very much GTB-based, and the front suspension was fabricated tube wishbones top and bottom, with Koni adjustable dampers. This car certainly meant business—with its double rear wishbones, anti-roll bars front and rear, massive vacuum-assisted ventilated discs clamped by new Ferrari/Brembo calipers, and cast magnesium used for lightweight manifolding and cam covers (look out for the red paint). When *Road & Track* tested the 288 in March 1986, they recorded times of 5 seconds for 0–60 mph, 11 seconds for 0–100, and burned up a quarter mile in 14.1 seconds, with a terminal speed of 113 mph! The top speed attained was 180 mph.

All in all, the total figure of 288 GTOs produced is thought to be 272, although Ferrari seem to think the figure's nearer 255. Thus, the appearance of Ferrari's new 288 GTO kept the enthusiasts happy and the world's motoring press scribbling, which left Ferrari to busy themselves on its further development—the GTO Evoluzione.

Their timing, for once, was off. Actually, unfortunate, would probably be a fairer way of putting it. After all, how were they to know that Group B racing, the class for which they were preparing this super new GTO, was about to be banned. They didn't, but it was. As it turned out, this was not as unfortunate as first appears, for we may owe thanks for the F40 to the people who banned Group B. You may wonder why Ferrari didn't just enter the Evoluzione in Group C, but if you do, you obviously don't understand the Ferrari racing principle—if it doesn't look like you're going to win, don't enter. Group C racing in the mid-1980s, as we all know, had powerful Porsches jostling with equally impressive Jags, both of which Ferrari and their Evoluzione had no chance of

The GTO has a longer wheelbase than the GTB to accommodate an in-line engine/transmission arrangement

beating. So, the **GTO** Evoluzione died a death. Or did it?

Well, the only one ever made did, but it's quite obvious that its spirit lived on. The engine used in the Evoluzione was based on the 288, which Ferrari acknowledge was the base for the F40 V8. It possessed the same internal dimensions as the 288, but had a higher compression ratio, and greater valve lift and timing overlap. It had bigger turbos and a free breathing eight-throttle Weber fuel injection system, all of which added up to produce 650 bhp at 7800 rpm.

Due to its short life span, there are really no figures for performance. Although *Autocar* were fortunate enough to get their hands on it for the only outside, uncamouflaged, track test, they were not invited to push the car to its limits. Ferrari chose the location, Imola, or the Autodroma Dino Ferrari—how appropriate. They laid on a team of ten mechanics, Ralph Pinto one of their chief testers, and plenty of back-up Michelin rubber. Although *Autocar* did not compare it to the 288—they knew one was a racer, and the other really a road car, they said, just by explaining that, that the Evoluzione was seriously quick. Factory estimates on top speed lurked around the 230 mph mark.

Like the phoenix rising from the ashes, the F40 appeared as if by magic, within a year of Enzo expressing his birthday wishes. Nobody at the time seemed that bothered about where this miraculous beast had come from. The ultimate Ferrari simply appeared. However, it wasn't just a 'new rabbit-old hat' trick, but a magical resurrection of something great that had gone before, in this case, the GTO Evoluzione.

One thing's for sure, with hindsight, the chaps at Ferrari knew way back what was afoot. Giovanni Razelli hinted when telling *Autocar* about the Evoluzione in 1986: 'the light bodywork materials such as those used on the Evoluzione will find their way into our production cars soon.'

I don't think anybody realized how soon. The F40 is the ultimate GTO Evoluzione, and that, contrary to being against Enzo's wishes, is exactly what he had wanted. A car to celebrate 40 years of racing and production Ferraris, and what better than a car that utilized everything learnt on both road and track in all those years. No wonder it is a special car.

Pininfarina reportedly found considerable difficulty in styling the rear door jambs and wheel arches of the GTO—clearly they succeeded in overcoming the problems

THE F40

According to Ferrari Automobili, June 1986 was the time that Enzo Ferrari decided he wanted the F40 built. At exactly the same time, the decision was taken to ban World Championship Group B racing. So, the GTO Evoluzione, which had started life as a racing car designed to spend all its time on the track, suddenly became Ferrari's greatest road car. Not so much a birthday celebration, as a clever decision and a quick name change. Until very late in the day, the car was called Le Mans—that sounds pretty race-like to me, but 'Ferrari 40' (for an incredibly expensive half-race car with no racing future) sounds much more acceptable. That's why the F40 logo was, even by Ferrari's admission, a very hasty design. However, credit where credit's due, the timing for a 200+ mph production road car (bearing in mind the arrival of Porsche's 959) was perfect. That's a good enough reason, and the birthday celebration was the perfect excuse for such a lavish project.

As we have already seen, the Evoluzione didn't need much work doing to it to produce the F40; they had all the basics there at least, the shape and the engine being left virtually unaltered. It is interesting to note that the Evoluzione was built in collaboration with Michelotto. In fact, prototypes bearing a remarkable resemblance to the F40 were appearing around the world in mid-1987. One turned up at Donington Park in September 1987 (with Henk Koel, a Scuderia Ferrari driver, behind the wheel) and was acknowledged as the 308 GT/M. Two other examples were said to be in Belgium and Italy—was the Italian one the GTO Evoluzione?

Michelotto appear to have designed much of the aerodynamic body, and Pininfarina merely added the finishing touches. It also seems as if Ferrari had the F40 (or LM) prototypes dotted all over the world, and were gaining important experience on the track. By denying any affiliation

A celebration of 40 years worth of Ferraris—the F40 sits outside the factory

Undeniably a masterpiece

with it, or Michelotto, the rumour was sustained—the general opinion was that this was bound to be the case, as Ferrari could well be creating their own workhorse. They were. And it was right under everybody's nose.

Whether the body was designed by Pininfarina or Michelotto, it's undeniably a masterpiece, combining new technology with elegance and style. It's instantly recognizable, and although it's got many more straight lines than the previous GTOs, it still gives the impression of an inspired and free-flowing pen.

The entire body of the F40 is made from panels of Kevlar—a synthetic Du Pont material. It can be used in various forms, mats, fabric, or a combination of the two. The composite body is made from two outer skins that are glued to a central core of honeycomb. Thus, it's very strong and extremely light.

The panels' strength is also boosted by thermosetting resins with which the F40's skin is impregnated. These are cured in a pressurized oven and become solid pieces of immense strength. This process is utilized on the door openings, floor, spare wheel container, scuttle, and firewall, although this also contains aluminium. Two of the panels that make up the body are much larger and more complex than the others, these being the front and rear hoods, then there's the roof, the doors, the underside of the tail, the door sills, near sides and dashboard cover. The cost of producing a body in this way is expensive and requires a skilled workforce, but the process is well suited for limited production. Apart from the benefits of low weight and strength (when all panels are glued to the steel-tube frame, the rigid structure is three times stronger than a conventional frame), the moulds and dies required are much cheaper than for metal bodywork.

The F40 is, without doubt, a race car looking for somewhere to race

81

Every aspect of the F40 oozes functional race-car styling

Inside the rigid bodyshell, the passenger area is simple and efficient; the spartan upholstery leaves much of the composite body skin on display in true racing tradition. If those two torso-hugging red bucket seats (choose from three sizes) with their four-point harnesses don't put you in the racing mood, then the Momo wheel, drilled pedals, huge switches, speedometer that reads up to 360 kph, rev counter (7750 limit), water thermometer, boost pressure indicator and exposed electrical systems should set the adrenalin flowing. But Ferrari may have taken the racing theme a little too far—the doors, which open and close by means of a pull inside the door skin, are difficult to shut, and the perspex windows don't really open. That must be annoying if you've just spent a fortune on a road car. Air conditioning is an optional extra!

From the nose with it's three main intakes, the sides with ducts for cooling the rear brakes and sending air to the intercooler, the compressor inlet, heat exchangers and gearbox oil cooler (!), to the rear end with its heavily ventilated perspex hood, the whole bodyshell is an elaborate

Testing time. Will this be the only type of track workout the F40 sees?

The pistons and rods of the F40's V8 engine are matched to their own individual cylinder bores

cooling system. There are three exhaust outlets, one for each bank of cylinders, and one in the middle for wastegate emissions.

A GTO tradition, started by the 250 GTO in the 1960s, of three slightly angled ducts in the bodywork just behind the rear wheels, was repeated on the 288 GTO in 1984, re-appeared on the GTO Evoluzione (but with an additional slot), and made five when the F40 prototype appeared. At the Turin Show of 1988, both Ferrari and Pininfarina had F40s on their stands, but a closer look revealed only four slots on Pininfarina's version—just like the missing Evoluzione—and this was the arrangement that was eventually to appear on the production versions of the car. In Pininfarina's brochure for the Turin Show, they say (apart from claiming Turin as the venue for its first appearance), 'built and conceived by Ferrari to experiment with possible production ideas'.

The all-independent parallel-arm suspension has been designed to make best use of the ultra-low-profile tyres, which have been derived directly from the F1 cars. Made by Pirelli and called P ZERO, they have been introduced on the

The engine gradually assumes shape; here the heads have been added to the block

F40s. Their ZR coding indicates that they are suitable for the highest speeds attainable by the car. They have a distinctive asymmetrical tread design, and the ultra-low profile allows the use of 17 in. rims.

Each suspension assembly consists of two near-horizontal arms with helical springs and Koni hydraulic shocks, and there is a stabilizer bar for each axle. The distance between the body of the F40 and the road can be set at one of three levels. The highest level can be set manually for moving the car at low speeds up steep inclines, and the body will be returned automatically to the middle position when the car starts to accelerate when travelling in excess of 130 kph, the F40 will adopt another position relative to the ground that suits the high speeds and minimizes drag. These changes are controlled by an electronic device that compares the speed and height, then alters the latter accordingly by means of an electric pump that is connected to the hydraulic fluid valves in the dampers. There is a safety override that cuts in to avoid height changes if the speed is oscillating at the alteration point.

The braking system comes straight from the Evoluzione and comprises huge 330 mm discs that are ventilated internally by radial fins, as well as many axial holes. Only the area that the friction pads bear against is cast-iron, the rest being weight-saving light alloy. The light alloy calipers have four pistons each, two on either side, with the handbrake having its own separate set on the rear discs. There is no servo-assistance, so the driver has that direct feel, although they've tried to minimize the amount of strength you'll need to operate them—42 kg of pressure will provide a deceleration of 1 g.

Twin fuel tanks with a total capacity of 120 litres are of aeronautical origin and made from special rubber, while a foam-filling stops fuel sloshing about uncontrollably. They are serviced by beautiful filler caps that remind one of Cartier tank watches, but quick-operation racing-type caps are available on request—who said Ferrari weren't interested in seeing their little baby race?

So, what is the final formula for this remarkable car? It's all listed below in an easy reference table. I hope no one objects to my saving both of us a lot of time and trouble.

ENGINE
Rear, centrally-mounted, longitudinal axis, watercooled. Otto cycle

Cylinders 8 in 90-degree Vee
        Single capacity 367.03 cc
        Total capacity 2936.00 cc
Bore and stroke 82 × 69.5 mm
Compression ratio 7.8:1
Max power 351.5 kW (478 bhp DIN) at 7000 rpm
Max torque 577 Nm (58.8 kgm) at 4000 rpm
Valve gear Two overhead cams per bank, toothed belt drive, four valves per cylinder
Carburation Electronic Weber-Marelli fuel injection with two IHI turbos
Ignition Electronic, distributorless

CHASSIS AND BODY
Steel tubing space frame, reinforced with composite panels, body made entirely of Kevlar

Overleaf
The turbo wastegate; note the cooling fins

Right
One of the two Japanese IHI turbos

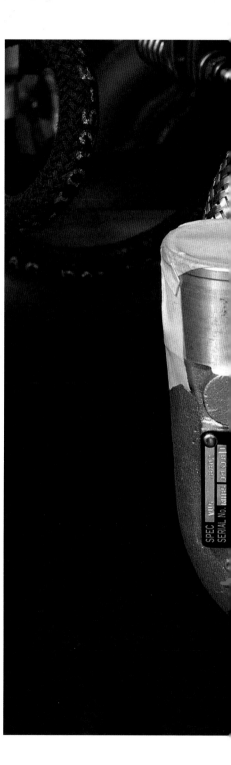

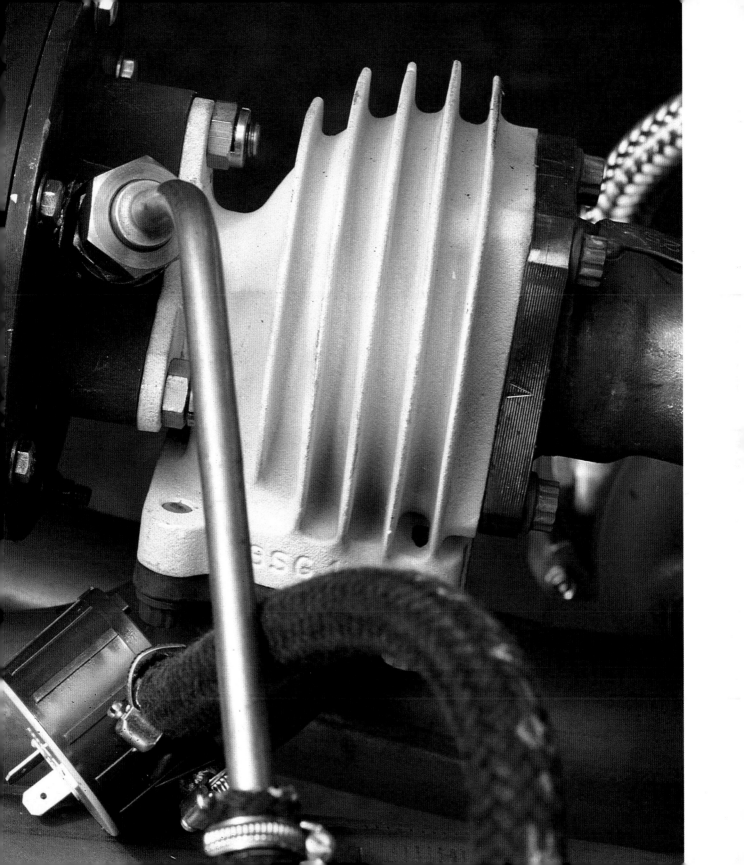

The complete engine assembly ready for mating to the transmission

TRANSMISSION
Rear-wheel-drive, engine in unit with gearbox and limited-slip diff. Five speeds, all synchro, and reverse. Non-synchro available on request. Reduction from engine to gearbox: 1333:1

Gear ratios First, 2.769:1; second, 1.722:1; third, 1.227:1; fourth, 0.963:1; fifth, 0.766:1; reverse, 2.461:1. Final belt drive, 2.727:1
Front suspension Independent, transverse arms, coil springs, telescopic dampers
Rear suspension Independent, transverse arms, coil springs, telescopic dampers
Anti-roll bars front and rear
Steering Rack-and-pinion
Brakes Four ventilated discs, dual hydraulic system
Tyres 245/40 ZR 17–335/35 ZR; pressure 2.5–3.0 bar
Wheelbase 2.45 m
Track 1.594 m, front; 1.610 m, rear
Length 4.43 m

Components of the gearbox and final drive

Width 1.98 m
Height 1.13 m (variable)
Weight Empty, 1100 kg; loaded—1400 kg plus 94 kg of fuel
Battery 12 volt, 65 amp/hour; generator 70 amp

A TRIP ROUND THE TRACK

Sometimes I feel lucky, and sometimes I don't. I wasn't
particularly chuffed to be in hospital having glass gouged from
my wrist and stitches sewn into place due to an unfortunate
accident with the front door. Ordinarily, it might have made
a dull day interesting. Not today; I was supposed to be on a
plane from Heathrow to East Midlands airport, it was
Thursday 26 January 1989, and I had work to do.

   Work? Not really, *Fast Lane* magazine wanted to try a new
concept in reader involvement, and they wanted me to help.
They classed it as a day's work; I saw it as the chance of a
lifetime. The idea was simple; hire Donington Park for the

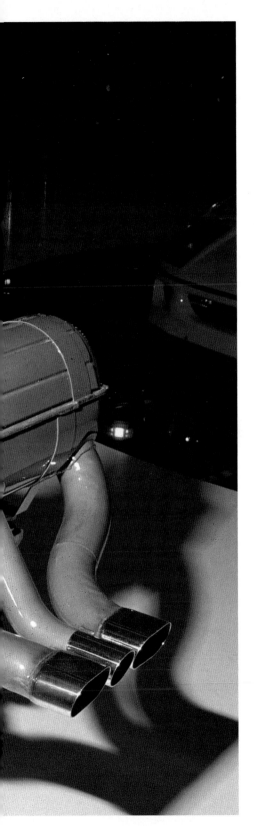

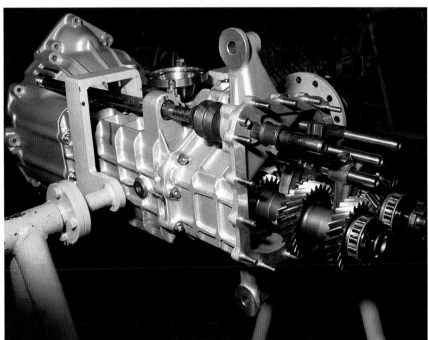

day; gather a selection of automobiles (from the lowliest Daihatsu to the holiest Ferrari); put Mark Hales (deputy editor) behind the wheel; wire up Beki in the passenger seat; thrash all six cars; tape the ensuing shrieks and whirrs whilst hopefully recording some decent commentary; run off a few thousand copies; add a pull-out section and give it all away in their April issue.

Simple. Except I was in casualty, and I'd lost a lot of blood. I missed the plane. I cried. I couldn't drive. Did I feel lucky? Definitely. Before I knew what had happened, I'd got a cab home, rung Donington and booked myself on the first flight in the morning—5.00 am. No problem. I'd be there. That's the power of the Ferrari F40.

The other five cars lined up for testing were mere hurdles to be overcome—a Daihatsu Charade GTti, an Escort XR3i, an Audi Quattro, a Sierra Cosworth, and a Porsche 911 Club Sport. Yes, we were behaving like spoilt children, but it was difficult to concentrate on any of them when every lap or so there was a glimpse of a beautiful red blurr hurtling around

Left
Complete engine and transmission assembly, including exhaust, ready for installation

Above
The assembled gearbox

the track, having just arrived from its home in London. Nick Mason, a rightfully proud owner, was getting his baby used to the track. Mr Hales and myself were desperados with little restraint or patience.

Finally, we were inside. I was wriggling myself into the dense sliver of a composite bucket seat, and it seemed to be hugging me back. Suddenly, I was locked in, and Nick was smiling knowingly as he helped with the four-point harness. Already I knew that this ride was going to be somewhat akin to a roller-coaster—but with no guarantee of staying on the rails. Mark and I kept looking at each other, we couldn't stop grinning. But how did he feel? This was a fortune's worth of Ferrari, and he was just about to push it to its limits.

'Are you nervous?' I asked, silently thinking, 'Well at least

Above
Though bright red, the cam cover is an understated indicator of the engine's maker

Left
The F40's V8, a masterpiece of engineering

Right
Composite duct directs cooling air to the brakes—red painted wheels are for rolling car around in factory only

Below
Details of the front bulkhead, showing the brake master cylinder, cooling pipes and front framework

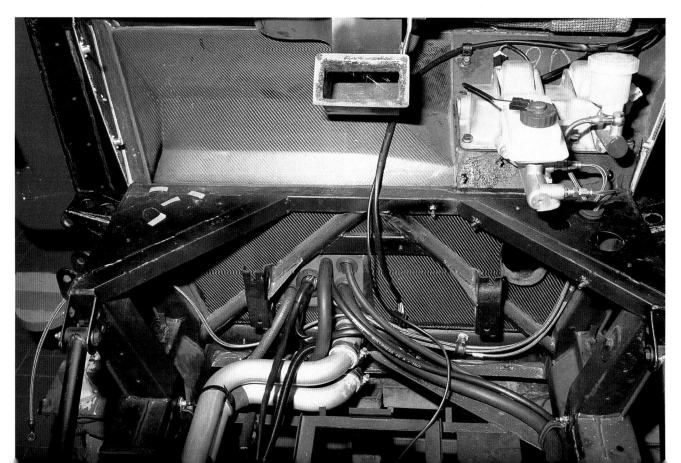

Left
The prototype F40 had five louvres in the rear wing, whereas the production version has four

Overleaf
The prototype had these swoopy door mirrors that never made it into production

you're in control mate; Mr Mason and I are now virtually helpless.' I looked around for Nick and spotted him aimlessly wandering off for a coffee, looking like a man without a worry in the world. Did he trust the car? Us?

'Look,' he had said to Mark earlier, 'it's here to be used, and if you think you can get on top of it, then you must be very serious indeed. Just take it when you're ready.' Nick believes that if you own a sports car, you have an almost moral duty to ensure that it is used as such. He put us at ease. At ease? Not quite, but then Mr Hales pushed the starter, and no drug on earth could have made me feel better.

The starter whirred somewhere behind us, and **478 bhp** rumbled and then hummed its way to life. The first surprise was that this one ticked-over as smoothly as the one straight out of the tuning bay in Turin, accompanied by those beautiful whirrs and hums. Then we were out on the track and stones were flicking up under the wheels, but that was the only noise interrupting pure sound—an **F40** heard from within the grey-felted cockpit, rumbling and roaring its way around a race track. Although both Mark and myself had jobs to do, which entailed talking at this point, as the tyres warmed and the rattle of stones receded, the pure sound was left uninterrupted as we remained speechless and the Ferrari hummed on. Dumbstruck and not even in third.

Mark allowed a lap or two to get used to the basic feel of the car, and to build up to full speed. Those huge ventilated Brembo discs needed some warming, Nick had done some of the groundwork, but the first time we needed them in a hurry, the servo-less grumbling and grinding came as a bit of a shock. We were up to speed, or as fast as we could hope for on the undulating, decidedly slippery, wet Donington track. Pure sound had been joined by the glorious whoosh of air as it swooped over (and into) the nose, over our heads, down the sides into the cooling ducts, and down across the perspex rear window/engine cover, which smoothes the flow to that distinctive rear spoiler (which gives the car downforce and stability at 150+ mph). The noise was quite unbelievable.

I watched as Mark seemed to use all the strength in his left leg to depress that solid $8\frac{1}{2}$ in. twin-plate clutch. Hydraulically-assisted it might be, but it still requires a Herculean shove. The right arm also looked like it needed a few biceps to guide the gear-shift through the GTO-derived aluminium gate. I looked up. We were nearly at the end of Starkeys Straight, and the chicane came next, so it was down from the high 130s at the end of the straight with those grumbling brakes—in good time, second gear through the bends, stomp on the throttle, and out with a whoosh and a wheelspin. Into third, up to the mid-120s, down towards Redgate, second again as we entered the fairly tight right— understeer found itself corrected by turbo boost, and as the rear end ran wide on the slippery surface, Mark's foot stomped down on the drilled alloy throttle pedal, then off, then on as he kept the boost flowing, but checked the

Making a hit at the Turin Motor Show

From every angle the F40 is powerfully stylish

wheelspin. We slid onwards to Holly Wood and beyond. But the **F40** was forgiving; braking and cornering at the same time didn't leave us out of control, but wheelspin, as Mark pointed out, was a danger.

'More revs equals more boost, equals more power, and if one wheel bites, it'll turn you whichever way into the wall.'

Fortunately for us, such an incident did not occur. We came close though. McLeans Corner, which is actually tighter than the Old Hairpin, turns through 90 degrees to the right, and for our last lap, Mr Hales wanted to make it count (as if the previous laps hadn't). In second, early throttle, and the equation came to life. More boost, more power, wheelspin, and we weren't in a tactical slide either. The revs had shot up. Mark had run out of hands—his right had gone full circle left—but as his foot came up, and the revs dropped, the car shifted back into line and we breathed again.

A race car with nowhere to race? The appointments of the F40 owe much to a competition-inspired specification

We whooshed, grumbled, screamed, whirred and roared around for a couple more laps, then eased back to home base as the brakes came off the boil and the turbos gasped. Engine cut, and the car gently clicked and ticked as metal started cooling and contracting. All Mr Hales and myself seemed capable of was uttering the words immortalized by Peter Fonda in *Easy Rider*—Wow .... wow!

So, that is the F40, and looking back over Ferrari's V8 production, from the Dino-inspired 308 to this, the ultimate, one gets a strange feeling that it was all a huge, brilliantly orchestrated plan, with the F40 as the ultimate celebration, and Enzo father of them all. His own 90th birthday celebrations, the same year as the company's 40th, and the launch of the F40 all fitted in so neatly. In a strange way, even Ferrari's death seemed timely; like the grandfather who clings to life just long enough to gather his family around him. The F40 was Enzo's final offspring, and a celebration of all Ferraris, past and present, racing and production. The ultimate cross-bred prancing horse. Enzo Ferrari must have died a happy man.

The ultimate road-going Ferrari about to be pushed to its limits

A Ferrari-powered Lancia

So far, we've looked at the more glamorous, better known applications of the Ferrari V8 engine, but it has been used as a powerplant in other production Ferraris and in one-off vehicles too, as the pictures in this chapter will show.

In 1973, a significant addition was made to the Ferrari stable with the introduction of the Mondial 8. This Pininfarina-styled 2+2 resurrected the name of a four-cylinder Ferrari sports-racer from the mid-1950s.

The Mondial 8 was a genuine attempt at providing a practical four-seat sports car with the sleek appearance expected of a Ferrari. It was based on the mechanics of the fuel-injected 308s and had a unique feature that had not been seen on any Ferrari before. This was a removable subframe that carried the engine, transmission and rear suspension as one assembly, making servicing that much easier.

In 1982, the Mondial 8 received the four-valve version of the V8 engine and became known as the Mondial quattrovalvole, while in 1983 a cabriolet version was introduced.

The latest production Ferrari to receive the V8 is the 348, which was announced at Frankfurt in September 1989. Styled once again by Pininfarina, the 348 is a two-seat sports car with a longitudinal, mid-mounted V8 engine of 3405 cc capacity. Like others before it, it is available in Berlinetta (tb) and Spyder (ts) versions, the 't' in the designation referring to the fact that the car features a transverse gearbox. This is not a new idea—the D50 racers inherited from Lancia in the 1950s had such arrangements.

Mention of Lancia brings us full circle in the Ferrari V8 story, for Lancia's high-performance, Thema 8.32 receives its motive power from a version of the very Ferrari V8 engine that has been the central theme of this book.

The sleekness of the Mondial is maintained at the front with twin pop-up headlights and flasher units let into the bumper

Left
*The subject of some criticism, the air
intakes on the Mondial were eventually
finished in a colour to match the rest of the
bodywork, making them less obtrusive*

Above
*Martin Hutchings puts his 1983/4 Mondial
through its paces at a Ferrari Owners'
Club meeting at Castle Coombe*

Overleaf
A reflection of the stylist's craft

Below
The sumptuous interior of the Mondial Qv
provides a reasonable amount of legroom
for rear-seat passengers

Right
The Mondial presented Pininfarina with
the problem of accommodating four people
in comfort in the 2 + 2 bodyshell, while
retaining the sleek appearance expected of
a Ferrari. They succeeded admirably

Right
The four-valve version of the V8 engine in Martin Hutchings' Mondial

Far right, above
Topless style—the Mondial Cabriolet

Far right, below
The well-appointed interior of the Mondial Cabriolet

Overleaf
Setting the pace for future V8 Ferraris?

Above
The PPG pace car was a styling exercise carried out by IDEA in Turin. It incorporates many features that could eventually see production

Above
*The Mondial provided the floorpan for the
PPG/Indy Car Racing Series pace car*

The 348's exciting body style exploits many aspects of the Testarossa's, in particular the grilles on the doors that channel cooling air to the rear radiator intakes

The 348 is not just a beautiful car—it can accelerate from a standstill to 100 kph in 5.6 seconds, will cover 1000 m from a standing start in 25.6 seconds and has a maximum speed of over 275 kph

Overleaf
The 3.4 litre V8 engine in Ferrari's 348— the first Ferrari for the 1990s. The engine is mounted longitudinally and connected to a new transverse gearbox—an echo from the past, since a transverse gearbox was also used in the Ferrari/Lancia D50 (see Chapter 1)

As with so many other Ferraris, the styling of the 348 is the product of the skilled craftsmen at Pininfarina

The front end styling of the two-seat 348 echoes famous Ferraris of the past—the 375MM, 196P, 275LM, the 330P3 and, of course, the F40

The wheel comes full circle, Lancia's luxury, high-performance four-door saloon, the 8.32, relies on Ferrari V8 power

The Ferrari V8 engine has even taken to
the waves—three were used to power
Martini's offshore powerboat racer